Community Helpers

Park Rangers

by Mary Firestone

Consultant:
Luke Lukas
Wilderness Program Coordinator
Vermilion College, Ely, Minnesota

Bridgestone Books
an imprint of Capstone Press
Mankato, Minnesota

Bridgestone Books are published by Capstone Press
151 Good Counsel Drive, P.O. Box 669, Mankato, Minnesota 56002
http://www.capstone-press.com

Library of Congress Cataloging-in-Publication Data
Firestone, Mary.
   Park rangers/by Mary Firestone.
   p.cm.—(Community helpers)
   Summary: A simple introduction to the work park rangers do, discussing where they
work, what tools they use, and how they are important to the communities they serve.
   Includes bibliographical references and index.
   ISBN 0-7368-1615-1 (hardcover)
   1. Park rangers—Juvenile literature. 2. Park rangers—Vocational guidance—Juvenile
literature. [1. Park rangers. 2. Occupations.] I. Title. II. Community helpers (Mankato,
Minn.).
SB486.V62 F48 2003
363. 6'8'0922—dc21   2002011104

Editorial Credits
Heather Adamson, editor; Karen Risch, product planning editor; Patrick D. Dentinger,
      cover production designer; Alta Schaffer, photo researcher

Photo Credits
Dave G. Houser/Houserstock, Inc., 8
Index Stock Imagery/John Luke, 18
Kent & Donna Dannen, 14, 16, 20
Roche Jaune Pictures, Inc./Jeff Henry, cover, 4, 6, 10, 12

1 2 3 4 5 6 08 07 06 05 04 03

Table of Contents

Park Rangers

Park rangers work in national parks and state parks. Rangers protect forests, lakes, and grasslands. They teach safety and help people find campsites. Law enforcement rangers make sure people follow park rules. Interpretive rangers show park visitors how to treat wildlife.

What Park Rangers Do

Park rangers have many jobs. They teach visitors about plants and animals. Some rangers patrol parks watching for fires or sick animals. Some rangers lead hikes. Rangers remove branches and poison ivy from trails. They check in campers and explain park rules.

patrol
to check an area regularly

What Park Rangers Wear

Park rangers wear uniforms. These clothes are often tan, green, or gray. Rangers wear a hat to shade their faces from the sun. Some rangers wear shorts in warm weather. Some park rangers also carry guns.

Tools Park Rangers Use

Park rangers use many tools. They use computers to check weather reports and keep records. Rangers find their way with maps. They use chain saws to cut branches that block roads. Rangers use rescue equipment and first aid kits to help people who are hurt.

Park Rangers and Transportation

Park rangers use many kinds of transportation. They use four-wheel drive trucks on hills and slippery roads. They ride snowmobiles in winter. Rangers also use horses, boats, and ATVs. They may use helicopters or airplanes to view wildlife.

ATV

an all-terrain vehicle that can ride over many types of ground

How Park Rangers Learn

Most park rangers have college degrees. Rangers must learn how to take care of land through conservation and fire safety. Rangers learn about the plants and animals in their area. Some take classes in law enforcement.

Skills Park Rangers Need

Park rangers need many skills. They must know how to swim and paddle a canoe. Rangers use math to manage park costs. They also need to know first aid and fire safety. Some rangers have rescue skills.

People Who Help Park Rangers

All park employees help park rangers.
Grounds crews keep the buildings
clean and the grass trimmed. Other
workers help rangers plant seeds.
Some parks have campground hosts
who live in the parks all summer. They
watch over the campgrounds.

How Park Rangers Help Others

Park rangers protect wildlife so everyone can enjoy it. They keep park visitors safe. They warn campers of bad weather. Park rangers teach others how to take care of nature.

Hands On: Make a Tree Display

Park rangers learn the names of trees and flowers. You can learn the names of trees in your own yard. Then display them like a park ranger does.

What You Need

leaves, twigs, bark, and pine cones
books about trees
paste
poster board
markers

What You Do

1. Collect leaves, twigs, loose bark, or pine cones that have fallen from trees in your area. Do not pull items off trees.
2. Use a book about trees to identify where each item came from. Ask an adult if you need help.
3. Arrange the collection into groups by type of tree.
4. Paste the groups onto the poster board.
5. Write the name of the tree below each group.

You can use your poster to teach your friends the names of your neighborhood trees.

Words to Know

conservation (kahn-ser-VAY-shuhn)—to protect something from being wasted or lost

enforcement (en-FORSS-ment)—making sure a rule is followed; law enforcement rangers give out tickets and make visitors who break rules leave the park.

interpretive (in-TUR-pruh-tiv)—explaining how something works; interpretive rangers explain different kinds of plants and animals to park visitors.

transportation (transs-pur-TAY-shuhn)—a way to move from one place to another

Read More

Burby, Liza N. *A Day in the Life of a Park Ranger.* The Kids' Career Library. New York: PowerKids Press, 1999.

Flanagan, Alice K. *Exploring Parks with Ranger Dockett.* Our Neighborhood. New York: Children's Press, 1997.

Internet Sites

Track down many sites about Park Rangers.
Visit the FACT HOUND at http://www.facthound.com

IT IS EASY! IT IS FUN!

1) Go to http://www.facthound.com
2) Type in: 0736816151
3) Click on "FETCH IT" and FACT HOUND will find several links hand-picked by our editors.

Relax and let our pal FACT HOUND do the research for you!

Index